VICTORIAN LOVE POETRY

selected by
Thomas Blaikie

MACMILLAN

Note

Paul Taylor and Brenda Stephenson have helped enormously.
My thanks to them.

Throughout this book the poets are arranged alphabetically
and the poems are given in order of composition
for each poet.

T.B.

ISBN 0 333 38540 3

First published 1985 by
PAPERMAC
a division of Macmillan Publishers Limited
4 Little Essex Street London WC2R 3LF
and Basingstoke

Associated companies in Auckland, Delhi, Dublin, Gaborone,
Hamburg, Harare, Hong Kong, Johannesburg, Kuala Lumpur,
Lagos, Manzini, Melbourne, Mexico City, Nairobi, New York, Singapore
and Tokyo

Printed in Hong Kong

Contents

MATTHEW ARNOLD

Meeting

Again I see my bliss at hand,
The town, the lake are here;
My Marguerite smiles upon the strand,
Unaltered with the year.

I know that graceful figure fair,
That cheek of languid hue;
I know that soft, enkerchiefed hair,
And those sweet eyes of blue.

Again I spring to make my choice;
Again in tones of ire
I hear a God's tremendous voice:
'Be counselled, and retire.'

Ye guiding Powers who join and part,
What would ye have with me?
Ah, warn some more ambitious heart,
And let the peaceful be!

To Marguerite – Continued

Yes! in the sea of life enisled,
With echoing straits between us thrown,
Dotting the shoreless watery wild,
We mortal millions live *alone*.
The islands feel the enclasping flow,
And then their endless bounds they know.

But when the moon their hollows lights,
And they are swept by balms of spring,
And in their glens, on starry nights,
The nightingales divinely sing;
And lovely notes, from shore to shore,
Across the sounds and channels pour –

Oh! then a longing like despair
Is to their farthest caverns sent;
For surely once, they feel, we were
Parts of a single continent!
Now round us spreads the watery plain –
Oh might our marges meet again!

Who ordered, that their longing's fire
Should be, as soon as kindled, cooled?
Who renders vain their deep desire? –
A God, a God their severance ruled!
And bade betwixt their shores to be
The unplumbed, salt, estranging sea.

Absence

In this fair stranger's eyes of grey
Thine eyes, my love! I see.
I shiver; for the passing day
Had borne me far from thee.

This is the curse of life! that not
A nobler, calmer train
Of wiser thoughts and feelings blot
Our passions from our brain;

But each day brings its petty dust
Our soon-choked souls to fill,
And we forget because we must
And not because we will.

I struggle towards the light; and ye,
Once-longed-for storms of love!
If with the light ye cannot be,
I bear that ye remove.

I struggle towards the light – but oh,
While yet the night is chill,
Upon time's barren, stormy flow,
Stay with me, Marguerite, still!

Dover Beach

The sea is calm to-night.
The tide is full, the moon lies fair
Upon the straits; – on the French coast the light
Gleams and is gone; the cliffs of England stand,
Glimmering and vast, out in the tranquil bay.
Come to the window, sweet is the night-air!
Only, from the long line of spray
Where the sea meets the moon-blanch'd land,
Listen! you hear the grating roar
Of pebbles which the waves draw back, and fling,
At their return, up the high strand,
Begin, and cease, and then again begin,
With tremulous cadence slow, and bring
The eternal note of sadness in.

Sophocles long ago
Heard it on the Ægæan, and it brought
Into his mind the turbid ebb and flow
Of human misery; we
Find also in the sound a thought,
Hearing it by this distant northern sea.

The Sea of Faith
Was once, too, at the full, and round earth's shore
Lay like the folds of a bright girdle furl'd.
But now I only hear
Its melancholy, long, withdrawing roar,
Retreating, to the breath
Of the night-wind, down the vast edges drear
And naked shingles of the world.

Ah, love, let us be true
To one another! for the world, which seems
To lie before us like a land of dreams,
So various, so beautiful, so new,
Hath really neither joy, nor love, nor light,
Nor certitude, nor peace, nor help for pain;
And we are here as on a darkling plain
Swept with confused alarms of struggle and flight,
Where ignorant armies clash by night.

MATTHEW ARNOLD

The Buried Life

Light flows our war of mocking words, and yet,
Behold, with tears mine eyes are wet!
I feel a nameless sadness o'er me roll.
Yes, yes, we know that we can jest,
We know, we know that we can smile!
But there's something in this breast,
To which thy light words bring no rest,
And thy gay smiles no anodyne.
Give me thy hand, and hush awhile,
And turn those limpid eyes on mine.
And let me read there, love! thy inmost soul.

Alas! is even love too weak
To unlock the heart, and let it speak?
Are even lovers powerless to reveal
To one another what indeed they feel?
I knew the mass of men concealed
Their thoughts, for fear that if revealed
They would by other men be met
With blank indifference, or with blame reproved;
I knew they lived and moved
Tricked in disguises, alien to the rest
Of men, and alien to themselves – and yet
The same heart beats in every human breast!

But we, my love! – doth a like spell benumb
Our hearts, our voices? – must we too be dumb?
Ah! well for us, if even we,
Even for a moment, can get free
Our heart, and have our lips unchained;
For that which seals them hath been deep-ordained!
Fate, which foresaw
How frivolous a baby man would be –
By what distractions he would be possessed,
How he would pour himself in every strife,
And well-nigh change his own identity –
That it might keep from his capricious play
His genuine self, and force him to obey
Even in his own despite his being's law,
Bade through the deep recesses of our breast
The unregarded river of our life
Pursue with indiscernible flow its way;
And that we should not see
The buried stream, and seem to be
Eddying at large in blind uncertainty,
Though driving on with it eternally.

But often, in the world's most crowded streets,
But often, in the din of strife,
There rises an unspeakable desire
After the knowledge of our buried life;
A thirst to spend our fire and restless force
In tracking out our true, original course;
A longing to inquire
Into the mystery of this heart which beats
So wild, so deep in us – to know
Whence our lives come and where they go.
And many a man in his own breast then delves,
But deep enough, alas! none ever mines.

And we have been on many thousand lines,
And we have shown, on each, spirit and power;
But hardly have we, for one little hour,
Been on our own line, have we been ourselves –
Hardly had skill to utter one of all
The nameless feelings that course through our breast,
But they course on for ever unexpressed.
And long we try in vain to speak and act
Our hidden self, and what we say and do
Is eloquent, is well – but 'tis not true!
And then we will no more be racked
With inward striving, and demand
Of all the thousand nothings of the hour
Their stupefying power;
Ah yes, and they benumb us at our call!
Yet still, from time to time, vague and forlorn,
From the soul's subterranean depth upborne
As from an infinitely distant land,
Come airs, and floating echoes, and convey
A melancholy into all our day
Only – but this rare –
When a beloved hand is laid in ours,
When, jaded with the rush and glare
Of the interminable hours,
Our eyes can in another's eyes read clear,
When our world-deafened ear
Is by the tones of a loved voice caressed –
A bolt is shot back somewhere in our breast,
And a lost pulse of feeling stirs again
The eye sinks inward, and the heart lies plain,
And what we mean, we say, and what we would, we know.
A man becomes aware of his life's flow,
And hears its winding murmur; and he sees
The meadows where it glides, the sun, the breeze.

And there arrives a lull in the hot race
Wherein he doth for ever chase
That flying and elusive shadow, rest.
An air of coolness plays upon his face,
And an unwonted calm pervades his breast.
And then he thinks he knows
The hills where his life rose,
And the sea where it goes.

A Dream

Was it a dream? We sailed, I thought we sailed,
Martin and I, down a green Alpine stream,
Bordered, each bank, with pines; the morning sun,
On the wet umbrage of their glossy tops,
On the red pinings of their forest-floor,
Drew a warm scent abroad; behind the pines
The mountain-skirts, with all their sylvan change
Of bright-leafed chestnuts and mossed walnut-trees
And the frail scarlet-berried ash, began.
Swiss chalets glittered on the dewy slopes,
And from some swarded shelf, high up, there came,
Notes of wild pastoral music – over all
Ranged, diamond-bright, the eternal wall of snow.
Upon the mossy rocks at the stream's edge,
Backed by the pines, a plank-built cottage stood,
Bright in the sun; the climbing gourd-plant's leaves
Muffled its walls, and on the stone-strewn roof
Lay the warm golden gourds; golden, within,
Under the eaves, peered rows of Indian corn.
We shot beneath the cottage with the stream.
On the brown, rude-carved balcony, two forms
Came forth – Olivia's, Marguerite! and thine.
Clad were they both in white, flowers in their breast;
Straw hats bedecked their heads, with ribbons blue,
Which danced, and on their shoulders, fluttering, played.
They saw us, they conferred; their bosoms heaved,
And more than mortal impulse filled their eyes.
Their lips moved; their white arms, waved eagerly,
Flashed once, like falling streams; we rose, we gazed.

One moment, on the rapid's top, our boat
Hung poised – and then the darting river of Life
(Such now, methought, it was), the river of Life,
Loud thundering, bore us by; swift, swift it foamed,
Black under cliffs it raced, round headlands shone.
Soon the planked cottage by the sun-warmed pines
Faded – the moss – the rocks; us burning plains,
Bristled with cities, us the sea received.

WILFRID SCAWEN BLUNT

To Manon,
Comparing her to a Falcon

Brave as a falcon and as merciless,
With bright eyes watching still the world, thy prey,
I saw thee pass in thy lone majesty,
Untamed, unmated, high above the press.
The dull crowd gazed at thee. It could not guess
The secret of thy proud aërial way,
Or read in thy mute face the soul which lay
A prisoner there in chains of tenderness.
– Lo, thou art captured. In my hand to-day
I hold thee, and awhile thou deign'st to be
Pleased with my jesses. I would fain beguile
My foolish heart to think thou lovest me. See,
I dare not love thee quite. A little while
And thou shalt sail back heavenwards. Woe is me!

from *The Love-sonnets of Proteus*

11

St Valentine's Day

Today, all day, I rode upon the Down,
With hounds and horsemen, a brave company.
On this side in its glory lay the sea,
On that the Sussex Weald, a sea of brown.
The wind was light, and brightly the sun shone,
And still we galloped on from gorse to gorse.
And once, when checked, a thrush sang, and my horse
Pricked his quick ears as to a sound unknown.
I knew the spring was come. I knew it even
Better than all by this, that through my chase
In bush and stone and hill and sea and heaven
I seemed to see and follow still your face.
Your face my quarry was. For it I rode,
My horse a thing of wings, myself a god.

EMILY BRONTË

Untitled

If grief for grief can touch thee,
If answering woe for woe,
If any ruth can melt thee,
Come to me now!

I cannot be more lonely,
More drear I cannot be!
My worn heart throbs so wildly
'Twill break for thee.

And when the world despises,
When heaven repels my prayer,
Will not mine angel comfort?
Mine idol hear?

Yes, by the tears I've poured thee,
By all my hours of pain,
O I shall surely win thee,
Beloved, again!

from the 'Gondal' poems

EMILY BRONTË

R. Alcona to F. Brenzaida
[Remembrance]

Cold in the earth, and the deep snow piled above thee!
Far, far removed, cold in the dreary grave!
Have I forgot, my Only Love, to love thee,
Severed at last by Time's all-wearing wave?

Now, when alone, do my thoughts no longer hover
Over the mountains on Angora's shore;
Resting their wings where heath and fern-leaves cover
That noble heart for ever, ever more?

Cold in the earth, and fifteen wild Decembers
From those brown hills have melted into spring –
Faithful indeed is the spirit that remembers
After such years of change and suffering!

Sweet Love of youth, forgive if I forget thee
While the World's tide is bearing me along:
Sterner desires and darker hopes beset me,
Hopes which obscure but cannot do thee wrong.

No other Sun has lightened up my heaven;
No other Star has ever shone for me:
All my life's bliss from thy dear life was given –
All my life's bliss is in the grave with thee.

But when the days of golden dreams had perished
And even Despair was powerless to destroy,
Then did I learn how existence could be cherished,
Strengthened and fed without the aid of joy;

Then did I check the tears of useless passion,
Weaned my young soul from yearning after thine;
Sternly denied its burning wish to hasten
Down to that tomb already more than mine!

And even yet, I dare not let it languish,
Dare not indulge in Memory's rapturous pain;
Once drinking deep of that divinest anguish,
How could I seek the empty world again?

from the 'Gondal' poems

ROBERT BROWNING

Porphyria's Lover

The rain set early in tonight,
    The sullen wind was soon awake,
It tore the elm-tops down for spite,
    And did its worst to vex the lake:
    I listened with heart fit to break.
When glided in Porphyria; straight
    She shut the cold out and the storm,
And kneeled and made the cheerless grate
    Blaze up, and all the cottage warm;
    Which done, she rose, and from her form
Withdrew the dripping cloak and shawl,
    And laid her soiled gloves by, untied
Her hat and let the damp hair fall,
    And, last, she sat down by my side
    And called me. When no voice replied,
She put my arm about her waist,
    And made her smooth white shoulder bare,
And all her yellow hair displaced,
    And, stooping, made my cheek lie there,
    And spread, o'er all, her yellow hair,
Murmuring how she loved me – she
    Too weak, for all her heart's endeavour,
To set its struggling passion free
    From pride, and vainer ties dissever,
    And give herself to me for ever.

But passion sometimes would prevail,
    Nor could tonight's gay feast restrain
A sudden thought of one so pale
    For love of her, and all in vain:
    So, she was come through wind and rain.
Be sure I looked up at her eyes
    Happy and proud; at last I knew
Porphyria worshipped me; surprise
    Made my heart swell, and still it grew
    While I debated what to do.
That moment she was mine, mine, fair,
    Perfectly pure and good: I found
A thing to do, and all her hair
    In one long yellow string I wound
    Three times her little throat around,
And strangled her. No pain felt she;
    I am quite sure she felt no pain.
As a shut bud that holds a bee,
    I warily oped her lids: again
    Laughed the blue eyes without a stain.
And I untightened next the tress
    About her neck; her cheek once more
Blushed bright beneath my burning kiss:
    I propped her head up as before
    Only, this time my shoulder bore
Her head, which droops upon it still:
    The smiling rosy little head,
So glad it has its utmost will,
    That all it scorned at once is fled,
    And I, its love, am gained instead!
Porphyria's love: she guessed not how
    Her darling one wish would be heard.
And thus we sit together now,
    And all night long we have not stirred,
    And yet God has not said a word!

Meeting at Night

The grey sea and the long black land;
And the yellow half-moon large and low;
And the startled little waves that leap
In fiery ringlets from their sleep,
As I gain the cove with pushing prow,
And quench its speed i' the slushy sand.

Then a mile of warm sea-scented beach;
Three fields to cross till a farm appears;
A tap at the pane, the quick sharp scratch
And blue spurt of a lighted match,
And a voice less loud, through its joys and fears,
Than the two hearts beating each to each!

Love Among the Ruins

Where the quiet-coloured end of evening smiles,
  Miles and miles
On the solitary pastures where our sheep
  Half-asleep
Tinkle homeward through the twilight, stray or stop
  As they crop –
Was the site once of a city great and gay,
  (So they say)
Of our country's very capital, its prince
  Ages since
Held his court in, gathered councils, wielding far
  Peace or war.

Now, – the country does not even boast a tree,
 As you see,
To distinguish slopes of verdure, certain rills
 From the hills
Intersect and give a name to, (else they run
 Into one)
Where the domed and daring palace shot its spires
 Up like fires
O'er the hundred-gated circuit of a wall
 Bounding all
Made of marble, men might march on nor be pressed,
 Twelve abreast.

And such plenty and perfection, see, of grass
 Never was!
Such a carpet as, this summer-time, o'erspreads
 And embeds
Every vestige of the city, guessed alone
 Stock or stone –
Where a multitude of men breathed joy and woe
 Long ago;
Lust of glory pricked their hearts up, dread of shame
 Struck them tame;
And that glory and that shame alike, the gold
 Bought and sold.

Now, – the single little turret that remains
   On the plains,
By the caper over-rooted, by the gourd
   Overscored,
While the patching houseleek's head of blossom winks
   Through the chinks –
Marks the basement whence a tower in ancient time
   Sprang sublime,
And a burning ring, all round, the chariots traced
   As they raced
And the monarch and his minions and his dames
   Viewed the games.

And I know, while thus the quiet-coloured eve
   Smiles to leave
To their folding, all our many-tinkling fleece
   In such peace,
And the slopes and rills in undistinguished grey
   Melt away –
That a girl with eager eyes and yellow hair
   Waits me there
In the turret whence the charioteers caught soul
   For the goal,
When the king looked, where she looks now, breathless, dumb
   Till I come.

But he looked upon the city, every side,
   Far and wide,
All the mountains topped with temples, all the glades'
   Colonnades,
All the causeys, bridges, aqueducts, – and then,
   All the men!
When I do come, she will speak not, she will stand,
   Either hand
On my shoulder, give her eyes the first embrace
   Of my face,
Ere we rush, ere we extinguish sight and speech
   Each on each.

In one year they sent a million fighters forth
   South and North,
And they built their gods a brazen pillar high
   As the sky,
Yet reserved a thousand chariots in full force –
   Gold, of course
Oh heart! oh blood that freezes, blood that burns!
   Earth's returns
For whole centuries of folly, noise and sin!
   Shut them in,
With their triumphs and their glories and the rest!
   Love is best.

ROBERT BROWNING

Evelyn Hope

Beautiful Evelyn Hope is dead!
   Sit and watch by her side an hour.
That is her book-shelf, this her bed;
   She plucked that piece of geranium-flower,
Beginning to die too, in the glass;
   Little has yet been changed, I think:
The shutters are shut, no light may pass
   Save two long rays through the hinge's chink.

Sixteen years old when she died!
   Perhaps she had scarcely heard my name;
It was not her time to love; beside,
   Her life had many a hope and aim,
Duties enough and little cares,
   And now was quiet, now astir,
Till God's hand beckoned unawares, –
   And the sweet white brow is all of her.

Is it too late then, Evelyn Hope?
   What, your soul was pure and true,
The good stars met in your horoscope,
   Made you of spirit, fire and dew –
And, just because I was thrice as old
   And our paths in the world diverged so wide,
Each was naught to each, must I be told?
   We were fellow mortals, naught beside?

No, indeed! for God above
   Is great to grant, as mighty to make,
And creates the love to reward the love:
   I claim you still, for my own love's sake!
Delayed it may be for more lives yet,
   Through worlds I shall traverse, not a few:
Much is to learn, much to forget
   Ere the time be come for taking you.

But the time will come, – at last it will,
   When, Evelyn Hope, what meant (I shall say)
In the lower earth, in the years long still,
   That body and soul so pure and gay?
Why your hair was amber, I shall divine,
   And your mouth of your own geranium's red –
And what you would do with me, in fine,
   In the new life come in the old one's stead.

I have lived (I shall say) so much since then,
   Given up myself so many times
Gained me the gains of various men,
   Ransacked the ages, spoiled the climes;
Yet one thing, one, in my soul's full scope,
   Either I missed or itself missed me:
And I want and find you, Evelyn Hope!
   What is the issue? let us see!

I loved you, Evelyn, all the while.
   My heart seemed full as it could hold?
There was place and to spare for the frank young smile,
   And the red young mouth, and the hair's young gold.
So, hush, – I will give you this leaf to keep:
   See, I shut it inside the sweet cold hand!
There, that is our secret: go to sleep!
   You will wake, and remember, and understand.

A Serenade at the Villa

That was I, you heard last night,
　　When there rose no moon at all,
Nor, to pierce the strained and tight
　　Tent of heaven, a planet small:
Life was dead and so was light.

Not a twinkle from the fly,
　　Not a glimmer from the worm;
When the crickets stopped their cry,
　　When the owls forbore a term,
You heard music; that was I.

Earth turned in her sleep with pain,
　　Sultrily suspired for proof:
In at heaven and out again.
　　Lightning! – where it broke the roof,
Bloodlike, some few drops of rain.

What they could my words expressed,
　　O my love, my all, my one!
Singing helped the verses best,
　　And when singing's best was done,
To my lute I left the rest.

So wore night; the East was grey,
　　White the broad-faced hemlock-flowers:
There would be another day;
　　Ere its first of heavy hours
Found me, I had passed away.

What became of all the hopes,
    Words and song and lute as well?
Say, this struck – 'When life gropes
    Feebly for the path where fell
Light last on the evening slopes,

'One friend in that path shall be,
    To secure my step from wrong;
One to count night day for me,
    Patient through the watches long,
Serving most with none to see.'

Never say – as something bodes –
    'So, the worst has yet a worse!
When life halts 'neath double loads,
    Better the taskmaster's curse
Than such music on the roads!

'When no moon succeeds the sun,
    Nor can pierce the midnight's tent
Any star, the smallest one,
    While some drops, where lightning rent,
Show the final storm begun –

'When the fire-fly hides its spot,
    When the garden-voices fail
In the darkness thick and hot, –
    Shall another voice avail,
That shape be where these are not?

'Has some plague a longer lease,
    Proffering its help uncouth?
Can't one even die in peace?
    As one shuts one's eyes on youth,
Is that face the last one sees?'

Oh how dark your villa was,
   Windows fast and obdurate!
How the garden grudged me grass
   Where I stood – the iron gate
Ground its teeth to let me pass!

from *Andrea del Sarto*

(called 'The Faultless Painter')

In this monologue Andrea del Sarto addresses his wife, Lucrezia. The last extract
refers to the time he spent at the French court of Francis I.

I often am much wearier than you think,
This evening more than usual, and it seems
As if – forgive now – should you let me sit
Here by the window with your hand in mine
And look a half-hour forth on Fiesole,
Both of one mind, as married people use,
Quietly, quietly the evening through,
I might get up tomorrow to my work
Cheerful and fresh as ever. Let us try.
Tomorrow, how you shall be glad for this!
Your soft hand is a woman of itself,
And mine the man's bared breast she curls inside.

*   *   *

Nay, Love, you did give all I asked, I think –
More than I merit, yes, by many times.
But had you – oh, with the same perfect brow,
And perfect eyes, and more than perfect mouth,
And the low voice my soul hears, as a bird
The fowler's pipe, and follows to the snare –
Had you, with these the same, but brought a mind!
Some women do so. Had the mouth there urged
'God and the glory! never care for gain.
The present by the future, what is that?
Live for fame, side by side with Agnolo!
Rafael is waiting: up to God, all three!'
I might have done it for you. So it seems:
Perhaps not. All is as God over-rules.
Beside, incentives come from the soul's self;
The rest avail not. Why do I need you?
What wife had Rafael, or has Agnolo?
In this world, who can do a thing, will not;
And who would do it, cannot, I perceive:
Yet the will's somewhat – somewhat, too the power –
And thus we half-men struggle. At the end,
God, I conclude, compensates, punishes.
'Tis safer for me, if the award be strict,
That I am something underrated here,
Poor this long while, despised, to speak the truth.

*   *   *

A good time, was it not, my kingly days?
And had you not grown restless ... but I know –
'Tis done and past; 'twas right, my instinct said;
Too live the life grew, golden and not grey,
And I'm the weak-eyed bat no sun should tempt –
Out of the grange whose four walls makes his world.
How could it end in any other way?
You called me, and I came home to your heart.
The triumph was – reach and stay there; since
I reached it ere the triumph, what is lost?
Let my hands frame your face in your hair's gold,
You beautiful Lucrezia that are mine!

Two in the Campagna

I wonder do you feel today
    As I have felt since, hand in hand,
We sat down on the grass, to stray
    In spirit better through the land,
This morn of Rome and May?

For me, I touched a thought, I know,
    Has tantalized me many times,
(Like turns of thread the spiders throw
    Mocking across our path) for rhymes
To catch at and let go.

Help me to hold it! First it left
    The yellowing fennel, run to seed
There, branching from the brickwork' cleft,
    Some old tomb's ruin: yonder weed
Took up the floating weft,

Where one small orange cup amassed
    Five beetles, – blind and green they grope
Among the honey-meal: and last,
    Everywhere on the grassy slope
I traced it. Hold it fast!

The champaign with its endless fleece
    Of feathery grasses everwhere!
Silence and passion, joy and peace,
    An everlasting wash of air –
Rome's ghost since her decease.

Such life here, through such lengths of hours,
    Such miracles performed in play,
Such primal naked forms of flowers,
    Such letting nature have her way
While heaven looks from its towers!

How say you? Let us, O my dove,
    Let us be unashamed of soul,
As earth lies bare to heaven above!
    How is it under our control
To love or not to love?

I would that you were all to me,
    You that are just so much, no more.
Nor yours nor mine, nor slave nor free!
    Where does the fault lie? What the core
O' the wound, since wound must be?

I would I could adopt your will,
    See with your eyes, and set my heart
Beating by yours, and drink my fill
    At your soul's springs, – your part my part
In life, for good and ill.

No. I yearn upward, touch you close,
  Then stand away. I kiss your cheek,
Catch your soul's warmth, – I pluck the rose
  And love it more than tongue can speak –
Then the good minute goes.

Already how am I so far
  Out of that minute? Must I go
Still like the thistle-ball, no bar,
  Onward, whenever light winds blow,
Fixed by no friendly star?

Just when I seemed about to learn!
  Where is the thread now? Off again!
The old trick! Only I discern –
  Infinite passion, and the pain
Of finite hearts that yearn.

from *One Word More*

Browning is preoccupied with artists who have celebrated their lovers in a different medium from their usual and thus avoided a public expression of private feelings. Browning here refers to *Men and Women*, the volume in which this poem appears.

I shall never, in the years remaining,
Paint you pictures, no, nor carve you statues,
Make you music that should all-express me;
So it seems: I stand on my attainment.
This of verse alone, one life allows me;
Verse and nothing else have I to give you.
Other heights in other lives, God willing:
All the gifts from all the heights, your own, Love!

Yet a semblance of resource avails us –
Shade so finely touched, love's sense must seize it.
Take these lines, look lovingly and nearly,
Lines I write the first time and the last time.
He who works in fresco, steals a hair-brush,
Curbs the liberal hand, subservient proudly,
Cramps his spirit, crowds its all in little,
Makes a strange art of an art familiar,
Fills his lady's missal-marge with flowerets.
He who blows through bronze, may breathe through silver,
Fitly serenade a slumbrous princess.
He who writes, may write for once as I do.

Love, you saw me gather men and women,
Live or dead or fashioned by my fancy,
Enter each and all, and use their service,
Speak from every mouth, – the speech, a poem.
Hardly shall I tell my joys and sorrows,
Hopes and fears, belief and disbelieving:
I am mine and yours – the rest be all men's,
Karshish, Cleon, Norbert and the fifty.
Let me speak this once in my true person,
Not as Lippo, Roland or Andrea,
Though the fruit of speech be just this sentence:
Pray you, look on these my men and women,
Take and keep my fifty poems finished;
Where my heart lies, let my brain lie also!
Poor the speech; be how I speak, for all things.

*   *   *

This I say of me, but think of you, Love!
This to you – yourself my moon of poets!
Ah, but that's the world's side, there's the wonder,
Thus they see you, praise you, think they know you!
There, in turn I stand with them and praise you –
Out of my own self, I dare to phrase it.
But the best is when I glide from out them,
Cross a step or two of dubious twilight,
Come out on the other side, the novel
Silent silver lights and darks undreamed of,
Where I hush and bless myself with silence.

On the Cliff

I leaned on the turf,
I looked at a rock
Left dry by the surf;
For the turf, to call it grass were to mock:
Dead to the roots, so deep was done
The work of the summer sun.

And the rock lay flat
As an anvil's face:
No iron like that!
Baked dry; of a weed, of a shell, no trace:
Sunshine outside, but ice at the core,
Death's altar by the lone shore.

On the turf, sprang gay
With his films of blue,
No cricket, I'll say,
But a warhorse, barbed and chanfroned too,
The gift of a quixote-mage to his knight,
Real fairy, with wings all right.

On the rock, they scorch
Like a drop of fire
From a brandished torch
Fall two red fans of a butterfly:
No turf, no rock: in their ugly stead,
See, wonderful blue and red!

Is it not so
With the minds of men?
The level and low,
The burnt and bare, in themselves; but then
With such a blue and red grace, not theirs, –
Love settling unawares!

from James Lee's Wife

Eurydice to Orpheus

A Picture by Leighton

But give them me, the mouth, the eyes, the brow!
Let them once more absorb me! One look now
   Will lap me round for ever, not to pass
Out of its light, though darkness lie beyond:
Hold me but safe again within the bond
   Of one immortal look! All woe that was,
Forgotten, and all terror that may be,
Defied, – no past is mine, no future: look at me!

ELIZABETH BARRETT BROWNING

from *Sonnets from the Portuguese*

Can it be right to give what I can give?
To let thee sit beneath the fall of tears
As salt as mine, and hear the sighing years
Re-sighing on my lips renunciative
Through those infrequent smiles, which fail to live
For all thy adjurations? O my fears,
That this can scarce be right! We are not peers,
So to be lovers; and I own and grieve
That givers of such gifts as mine are, must
Be counted with the ungenerous. Out, alas!
I will not soil thy purple with my dust,
Nor breathe my poison on thy Venice-glass,
Nor give thee any love . . . which were unjust.
Beloved, I only love thee! let it pass.

*   *   *

ELIZABETH BARRETT BROWNING

If thou must love me, let it be for nought
Except for love's sake only. Do not say
'I love her for her smile . . her look . . her way
Of speaking gently, . . for a trick of thought
That falls in well with mine, and certes brought
A sense of pleasant ease on such a day' –
For these things in themselves, Beloved, may
Be changed, or change for thee, – and love so wrought,
May be unwrought so. Neither love me for
Thine own dear pity's wiping my cheeks dry,
Since one might well forget to weep who bore
Thy comfort long, and lose thy love thereby.
But love me for love's sake, that evermore
Thou may'st love on through love's eternity.

       *   *   *

Say over again and yet once over again
That thou dost love me. Though the word repeated
Should seem 'a cuckoo-song,' as thou dost treat it,
Remember never to the hill or plain,
Valley and wood, without her cuckoo-strain,
Comes the fresh Spring in all her green completed!
Beloved, I, amid the darkness greeted
By a doubtful spirit-voice, in that doubt's pain
Cry . . speak once more . . thou lovest! Who can fear
Too many stars, though each in heaven shall roll –
Too many flowers, though each shall crown the year?
Say thou dost love me, love me, love me – toll
The silver iterance! – only minding, Dear,
To love me also in silence, with thy soul.

       *   *   *

When we met first and loved, I did not build
Upon the event with marble. Could it mean
To last, a love set pendulous between
Sorrow and sorrow? Nay, I rather thrilled,
Distrusting ever light that seemed to gild
The onward path, and feared to overlean
A finger even. And, though I have grown serene
And strong since them, I think that God has willed
A still renewable fear . . O love, O troth . .
Lest these enclasped hands should never hold,
This mutual kiss drop down between us both
As an unowned thing, once the lips being cold.
And Love be false! if *he*, to keep one oath,
Must lose one joy by his life's star foretold.

SAMUEL BUTLER

[*Sonnet after Shakespeare*]

She was too kind, wooed too persistently,
Wrote moving letters to me day by day;
The more she wrote, the more unmoved was I,
The more she gave, the less could I repay.
Therefore I grieve not that I was not loved
But that, being loved, I could not love again.
I liked; but like and love are far removed;
And though I tried to love I tried in vain.
For she was plain and lame and fat and short,
Forty and over-kind. Hence it befell
That, though I loved her in a certain sort,
Yet did I love too wisely but not well.
Ah! had she been more beauteous or less kind
She might have found me of another mind.

JOHN CLARE

Mary

It is the evening hour,
    How silent all doth lie:
The horned moon she shows her face
    In the river with the sky.
Just by the path on which we pass,
The flaggy lake lies still as glass.

Spirit of her I love,
    Whispering to me
Stories of sweet visions as I rove,
    Here stop, and crop with me
Sweet flowers that in the still hour grew –
We'll take them home, nor shake off the bright dew.

Mary, or sweet spirit of thee,
    As the bright sun shines to-morrow
Thy dark eyes these flowers shall see,
    Gathered by me in sorrow,
In the still hour when my mind was free
To walk alone – yet wish I walked with thee.

JOHN CLARE

An Invite, to Eternity

Wilt thou go with me, sweet maid,
Say, maiden, wilt thou go with me
Through the valley-depths of shade,
Of night and dark obscurity;
Where the path has lost its way,
Where the sun forgets the day,
Where there's nor life nor light to see,
Sweet maiden, wilt thou go with me?

Where stones will turn to flooding streams,
Where plains will rise like ocean waves,
Where life will fade like visioned dreams
And mountains darken into caves,
Say, maiden, wilt thou go with me
Through this sad non-identity,
Where parents live and are forgot,
And sisters live and know us not?

Say, maiden, wilt thou go with me
In this strange death of life to be,
To live in death and be the same,
Without this life or home or name,
At once to be and not to be –
That was and is not – yet to see
Things pass like shadows, and the sky
Above, below, around us lie?

The land of shadows wilt thou trace,
And look – nor know each other's face;
The present mixed with reason gone,
And past and present all as one?
Say, maiden, can thy life be led
To join the living with the dead?
Then trace thy footsteps on with me;
We're wed to one eternity.

It is Love

It is love.
There's a mildness i' the air;
The fields are green & fair;
And sunbeams there
From above.
There is singing o' birds;
There is bleating o' herds;
Waters waving like curds;
What is love
But the landscapes o' spring sunny green o' the grove?
And the maid walking there Mary Dove?

Is it love
To admire what God's sending,
Charm on charm never ending,
Ever varying, unspending?
Look above.
Clouds, rocks rough and ragged,
Temples unhewed, and jagged,
Where currish man never begged.
What is love
But nature & truth over ocean & grove?
And that first boyish charm Mary Dove?

It is love.
While grass remains green,
Mary Dove,
And clouds sail in heaven above,
And flowers come wi' spring you'll be love,
Mary Dove.
Burnet buttons growed dark in that hour;
Purple fitch dangled on the thorn bower;
And each little weed had no flower but love.
In that little meadow, like joys from above,
Walks the poet's young fancy, the sweet Mary Dove.

ARTHUR HUGH CLOUGH

from *Amours de Voyage*

Claude, an intellectual young man, writes from Florence of his vacillating feelings for Mary.

CLAUDE TO EUSTACE

I am in love, meantime, you think; no doubt you would think so.
I am in love, you say; with those letters, of course, you would say
    so.
I am in love, you declare. I think not so; yet I grant you
It is a pleasure indeed to converse with this girl. Oh, rare gift,
Rare felicity, this! she can talk in a rational way, can
Speak upon subjects that really are matters of mind and of
    thinking,
Yet in perfection retain her simplicity; never, one moment,
Never, however you urged it, however you tempt her, consents to
Step from ideas and fancies and loving sensations to those vain
Conscious understandings that vex the minds of mankind.
No, though she talk, it is music; her fingers desert not the keys; 'tis
Song, though you hear in the song the articulate vocables
    sounded,
Syllabled singly and sweetly the words of melodious meaning.
    I am in love, you say: I do not think so, exactly.

ARTHUR HUGH CLOUGH

CLAUDE TO EUSTACE

There are two different kinds, I believe, of human attraction:
One which simply disturbs, unsettles, and makes you uneasy,
And another that poises, retains, and fixes and holds you.
I have no doubt, for myself, in giving my voice for the latter.
I do not wish to be moved, but growing where I was growing,
There more truly to grow, to live where as yet I had languished.
I do not like being moved: for the will is excited; and action
Is a most dangerous thing; I tremble for something factitious,
Some malpractice of heart and illegitimate process;
We are so prone to these things, with our terrible notions of duty

CLAUDE TO EUSTACE

Ah, let me look, let me watch, let me wait, unhurried,
    unprompted!
Bid me not venture on aught that could alter or end what is
    present!
Say not, Time flies, and Occasion, that never returns, is
    departing!
Drive me not out, ye ill angels with fiery swords, from my Eden,
Waiting, and watching, and looking! Let love be its own
    inspiration!
Shall not a voice, if a voice there must be, from the airs that
    environ,
Yea, from the conscious heavens, without our knowledge or
    effort,
Break into audible words? And love be its own inspiration?

ARTHUR HUGH CLOUGH

CLAUDE TO EUSTACE

Wherefore and how I am certain, I hardly can tell; but it *is* so.
She doesn't like me, Eustace; I think she never will like me.
It is my fault, as it is my misfortune, my ways are not her ways?
It is my fault, that my habits and modes are dissimilar wholly?
'Tis not her fault; 'tis her nature, her virtue, to misapprehend
    them:
'Tis not her fault; 'tis her beautiful nature, not ever to know me.
Hopeless it seems, – yet I cannot, though hopeless, determine to
    leave it:
She goes – therefore I go; she moves, – I move, not to lose her.

CLAUDE TO EUSTACE

Oh 'tisn't manly, of course, 'tisn't manly, this method of
    wooing;
'Tisn't the way very likely to win. For the woman, they tell you,
Ever prefers the audacious, the wilful, the vehement hero;
She has no heart for the timid, the sensitive soul; and for
    knowledge, –
Knowledge, O ye Gods! – when did they appreciate knowledge?
Wherefore should they, either? I am sure I do not desire it.
    Ah, and I feel too, Eustace, she cares not a tittle about me!
(Care about me, indeed! and do I really expect it?)
But my manner offends; my ways are wholly repugnant;
Every word that I utter estranges, hurts, and repels her;
Every moment of bliss that I gain, in her exquisite presence,
Slowly, surely, withdraws her, removes her, and severs her from
    me.
Not that I care very much! – any way I escape from the boy's own
Folly, to which I am prone, of loving where it is easy.
Not that I mind very much! Why should I? I am not in love, and
Am prepared, I think, if not by previous habit,
Yet in the spirit beforehand for this and all that is like it;
It is an easier matter for us contemplative creatures,
Us upon whom the pressure of action is laid so lightly;
We, discontented indeed with things in particular, idle,
Sickly, complaining, by faith, in the vision of things in general,
Manage to hold on our way without, like others around us,
Seizing the nearest arm to comfort, help, and support us.
Yet, after all, my Eustace, I know but little about it.
All I can say for myself, for present alike and for past, is,
Mary Trevellyn, Eustace, is certainly worth your acquaintance.
You couldn't come, I suppose, as far as Florence to see her?

AUSTIN DOBSON

To 'Lydia Languish'

'Il me faut des emotions.'
Blanche Amory

You ask me, Lydia, 'whether I,
If you refuse my suit, shall die.'
   (Now pray don't let this hurt you!)
Although the time be out of joint,
I should not think a bodkin's point
   The sole resource of virtue;
Nor shall I, though your mood endure,
Attempt a final Water-cure
   Except against my wishes;
For I respectfully decline
To dignify the Serpentine.
   And make *hors-d'œuvres* for fishes;
But if you ask me whether I
   Composedly can go,
Without a look, without a sigh,
   Why, then I answer – No.

'You are assured,' you sadly say
(If in this most considerate way
    To treat my suit your will is),
That I shall 'quickly find as fair
Some new Neaera's tangled hair –
    Some easier Amaryllis.'
I cannot promise to be cold
If smiles are kind as yours of old
    On lips of later beauties;
Nor can I, if I would, forget
The homage that is Nature's debt,
    While man has social duties;
But if you ask shall I prefer
    To you I honour so,
A somewhat visionary Her,
    I answer truly – No.

You fear, you frankly add, 'to find
In me too late the altered mind
    That altering Time estranges.'
To this I make response that we
(As physiologists agree)
    Must have septennial changes;
This is a thing beyond control,
And it were best upon the whole
    To try and find out whether
We could not, by some means, arrange
This not-to-be-avoided change
    So as to change together;
But, had you asked me to allow
    That you could ever grow
Less amiable than you are now –
    Emphatically – No.

But – to be serious – if you care
To know how I shall really bear
   This much discussed rejection,
I answer you: As feeling men
Behave, in best romances, when
   You outrage their affection; –
With that gesticulatory woe,
By which, as melodramas show,
   Despair is indicated;
Enforced by all the liquid grief
Which hugest pocket-handkerchief
   Has ever simulated;
And when, arrived so far, you say
   In tragic accents, 'Go',
Then, Lydia, then . . . I still shall stay,
   And firmly answer – No.

ERNEST DOWSON

Non Sum Qualis Eram Bonae Sub Regno Cynarae

Last night, ah, yesternight, betwixt her lips and mine
There fell thy shadow, Cynara! thy breath was shed
Upon my soul between the kisses and the wine;
And I was desolate and sick of an old passion,
    Yea, I was desolate and bowed my head:
I have been faithful to thee, Cynara! in my fashion.

All night upon mine heart I felt her warm heart beat,
Night-long within mine arms in love and sleep she lay;
Surely the kisses of her bought red mouth were sweet;
But I was desolate and sick of an old passion,
    When I awoke and found the dawn was gray:
I have been faithful to thee, Cynara! in my fashion.

I have forgot much, Cynara! gone with the wind,
Flung roses, roses riotously with the throng,
Dancing, to put thy pale, lost lilies out of mind;
But I was desolate and sick of an old passion,
    Yea, all the time, because the dance was long:
I have been faithful to thee, Cynara! in my fashion.

I cried for madder music and for stronger wine,
But when the feast is finished and the lamps expire,
Then falls thy shadow, Cynara! the night is thine;
And I am desolate and sick of an old passion,
    Yea, hungry for the lips of my desire:
I have been faithful to thee, Cynara! in my fashion.

Terre Promise

for Herbert P. Horne

Even now the fragrant darkness of her hair
Had brushed my cheek; and once, in passing by,
Her hand upon my hand lay tranquilly:
What things unspoken trembled in the air!

Always I know, how little severs me
From mine heart's country, that is yet so far;
And must I lean and long across a bar,
That half a word would shatter utterly?

Ah might it be, that just by touch of hand,
Or speaking silence, shall the barrier fall;
And she shall pass, with no vain words at all,
But droop into mine arms, and understand!

Seraphita

Come not before me now, O visionary face!
Me tempest-tost, and borne along life's passionate sea;
Troublous and dark and stormy though my passage be;
Not here and now may we commingle or embrace,
Lest the loud anguish of the waters should efface
The bright illumination of thy memory,
Which dominates the night: rest, far away from me,
In the serenity of thine abiding-place!

But when the storm is highest, and the thunders blare,
And sea and sky are riven, O moon of all my night!
Stoop down but once in pity of my great despair,
And let thine hand, though over late to help, alight
But once upon my pale eyes and my drowning hair,
Before the great waves conquer in the last vain fight.

Epigram

Because I am idolatrous and have besought,
With grievous supplication and consuming prayer,
The admirable image that my dreams have wrought
Out of her swan's neck and her dark, abundant hair:
The jealous gods, who brook no worship save their own,
Turned my live idol marble and her heart to stone.

ERNEST DOWSON

Chanson sans Paroles

In the deep violet air,
   Not a leaf is stirred;
   There is no sound heard,
But afar, the rare
   Trilled voice of a bird.

Is the wood's dim heart,
   And the fragrant pine,
   Incense, and a shrine
Of her coming? Apart,
   I wait for a sign.

What the sudden hush said,
   She will hear, and forsake,
   Swift, for my sake,
Her green, grassy bed:
   She will hear and awake!

She will hearken and glide,
   From her place of deep rest,
   Dove-eyed, with the breast
Of a dove, to my side:
   The pines bow their crest.

I wait for a sign:
    The leaves to be waved,
    The tall tree-tops laved
In a flood of sunshine,
    This world to be saved!

In the deep violet air,
    Not a leaf is stirred;
    There is no sound heard,
But afar, the rare
    Trilled voice of a bird.

GEORGE MEREDITH

from *Modern Love*

Modern Love was published in 1862. The poet had been deserted
by his wife in 1858. The sonnet-like sequence of poems concerns
a husband and wife living uneasily after the wife has taken a
lover. Later the husband acquires a mistress, the 'lost Lady' of
the third extract. The poems are mainly written from the
husband's point of view.

By this he knew she wept with waking eyes:
That, at his hand's light quiver by her head,
The strange low sobs that shook their common bed,
Were called into her with a sharp surprise,
And strangled mute, like little gaping snakes,
Dreadfully venomous to him. She lay
Stone-still, and the long darkness flowed away
With muffled pulses. Then, as midnight makes
Her giant heart of Memory and Tears
Drink the pale drug of silence, and so beat
Sleep's heavy measure, they from head to feet
Were moveless, looking through their dead black years,
By vain regret scrawled over the blank wall.
Like sculptured effigies they might be seen
Upon their marriage-tomb, the sword between;
Each wishing for the sword that severs all.

* * *

In our old shipwrecked days there was an hour,
When in the firelight steadily aglow,
Joined slackly, we beheld the red chasm grow
Among the clicking coals. Our library-bower
That eve was left to us: and hushed we sat
As lovers to whom Time is whispering.
From sudden-opened doors we heard them sing:
The nodding elders mixed good wine with chat.
Well knew we that Life's greatest treasure lay
With us, and of it was our talk, 'Ah, yes!
Love dies!' I said: I never thought it less.
She yearned to me that sentence to unsay.
Then when the fire domed blackening, I found
Her cheek was salt against my kiss, and swift
Up the sharp scale of sobs her breast did lift:–
Now am I haunted by that taste! that sound!

* * *

We saw the swallows gathering in the sky,
And in the osier-isle we heard them noise.
We had not to look back on summer joys,
Or forward to a summer of bright dye:
But in the largeness of the evening earth
Our spirits grew as we went side by side.
The hour became her husband and my bride.
Love that had robbed us so, thus blessed our dearth!
The pilgrims of the year waxed very loud
In multitudinous chatterings, as the flood
Full brown came from the West, and like pale blood
Expanded to the upper crimson cloud.
Love that had robbed us of immortal things,
This little moment mercifully gave,
Where I have seen across the twilight wave
The swan sail with her young beneath her wings.

Their sense is with their senses all mixed in,
Destroyed by subtleties these women are!
More brain, O Lord, more brain! or we shall mar
Utterly this fair garden we might win.
Behold! I looked for peace, and thought it near.
Our inmost hearts had opened, each to each.
We drank the pure daylight of honest speech.
Alas! that was the fatal draught, I fear.
For when of my lost Lady came the word,
This woman, O this agony of flesh!
Jealous devotion bade her break the mesh,
That I might seek that other like a bird.
I do adore the nobleness! despise
The act! She has gone forth, I know not where.
Will the hard world my sentience of her share?
I feel the truth; so let the world surmise.

He found her by the ocean's moaning verge,
Nor any wicked change in her discerned;
And she believed his old love had returned,
Which was her exultation, and her scourge.
She took his hand, and walked with him, and seemed
The wife he sought, though shadow-like and dry.
She had one terror, lest her heart should sigh,
And tell her loudly she no longer dreamed.
She dared not say, 'This is my breast: look in.'
But there's a strength to help the desperate weak.
That night he learned how silence best can speak
The awful things when Pity pleads for Sin.
About the middle of the night her call
Was heard, and he came wondering to the bed.
'Now kiss me, dear! it may be, now!' she said.
Lethe had passed those lips, and he knew all.

Thus piteously Love closed what he begat:
The union of this ever-diverse pair!
These two were rapid falcons in a snare,
Condemned to do the flitting of the bat.
Lovers beneath the singing sky of May,
They wandered once; clear as the dew on flowers:
But they fed not on the advancing hours:
Their hearts held cravings for the buried day.
Then each applied to each that fatal knife,
Deep questioning, which probes to endless dole.
Ah, what a dusty answer gets the soul
When hot for certainties in this our life! –
In tragic hints here see what evermore
Moves dark as yonder midnight ocean's force,
Thundering like ramping hosts of warrior horse,
To throw that faint thin line upon the shore!

COVENTRY PATMORE

Going to Church

Felix, in love with Honoria, meets her and her sister at church.

I found them, with exactest grace
    And fresh as Spring, for Spring attired;
And by the radiance in her face
    I saw she felt she was admired;
And, through the common luck of love,
    A moment's fortunate delay,
To fit the little lilac glove,
    Gave me her arm; and I and they
(They true to this and every hour,
    As if attended on by Time),
Enter'd the Church while yet the tower
    Was noisy with the finish'd chime.

    Her soft voice, singularly heard
        Beside me, in her chant, withstood
    The roar of voices, like a bird
        Sole warbling in a windy wood;
    And, when we knelt, she seem'd to be
        An angel teaching me to pray;

And all through the high Liturgy
   My spirit rejoiced without allay,
Being, for once, borne clearly above
   All banks and bars of ignorance,
By this bright spring-tide of pure love
   And floated in a free expanse,
Whence it could see from side to side,
   The obscurity from every part
Winnow'd away and purified
   By the vibrations of my heart

from The Angel of the House

Joy and Use

Can ought compared with wedlock be
   For use? But He who made the heart
To use proportions joy. What He
   Has join'd let no man put apart.
Sweet Order has its draught of bliss
   Graced with the pearl of God's consent,
Ten times delightful in that 'tis
   Considerate and innocent.
In vain Disorder grasps the cup;
   The pleasure's not enjoy'd but spilt,
And, if he stoops to lick it up,
   It only tastes of earth and guilt.
His sorry raptures rest destroys;
   To live, like comets, they must roam;
On settled poles turn solid joys,
   And sunlike pleasures shine at home.

from The Angel of the House

Beata

Of infinite Heaven the rays,
Piercing some eyelet in our cavern black,
Ended their viewless track
On thee to smite
Solely, as on a diamond stalactite,
And in mid-darkness lit a rainbow's blaze,
Wherein the absolute Reason, Power, and Love,
That erst could move
Mainly in me but toil and weariness,
Renounced their deadening might,
Renounced their undistinguishable stress
Of withering white,
And did with gladdest hues my spirit caress,
Nothing of Heaven in thee showing infinite,
Save the delight.

from *To the Unknown Eros*

COVENTRY PATMORE

The Azalea

There, where the sun shines first
Against our room,
She train'd the gold Azalea, whose perfume
She, Spring-like, from her breathing grace dispersed.
Last night the delicate crests of saffron bloom,
For this their dainty likeness watch'd and nurst,
Were just at point to burst.
At dawn I dream'd, O God, that she was dead,
And groan'd aloud upon my wretched bed,
And waked, ah, God, and did not waken her,
But lay, with eyes still closed,
Perfectly bless'd in the delicious sphere
By which I knew so well that she was near,
My heart to speechless thankfulness composed.
Till 'gan to stir
A dizzy somewhat in my troubled head –
It *was* the azalea's breath, and she *was* dead!
The warm night had the lingering buds disclosed,
And I had fall'n asleep with to my breast
A chance-found letter press'd
In which she said,
'So, till to-morrow eve, my Own, adieu!
Parting's well-paid with soon again to meet,
Soon in your arms to feel so small and sweet,
Sweet to myself that am so sweet to you!'

from *To the Unknown Eros*

Departure

It was not like your great and gracious ways!
Do you, that have nought other to lament,
Never, my Love, repent
Of how, that July afternoon,
You went,
With sudden, unintelligible phrase,
And frighten'd eye,
Upon your journey of so many days,
Without a single kiss, or a good-bye?
I knew, indeed, that you were parting soon;
And so we sate, within the low sun's rays,
You whispering to me, for your voice was weak,
Your harrowing praise.
Well, it was well,
To hear you such things speak,
And I could tell
What made your eyes a growing gloom of love,
As a warm South-wind sombres a March grove.
And it was like your great and gracious ways
To turn your talk on daily things, my Dear,
Lifting the luminous, pathetic lash
To let the laughter flash,
Whilst I drew near,
Because you spoke so low that I could scarcely hear.
But all at once to leave me at the last,
More at the wonder than the loss aghast,
With huddled, unintelligible phrase,
And frighten'd eye,
And go your journey of all days
With not one kiss, or a good-bye,
And the only loveless look the look with which you pass'd:
'Twas all unlike your great and gracious ways.

from To the Unknown Eros

A Farewell

With all my will, but much against my heart,
We two now part.
My Very Dear,
Our solace is, the sad road lies so clear.
It needs no art,
With faint, averted feet
And many a tear,
In our opposed paths to persevere.
Go thou to East, I West.
We will not say
There's any hope, it is so far away.
But, O, my Best,
When the one darling of our widowhead,
The nursling Grief,
Is dead,
And no dews blur our eyes
To see the peach-bloom come in evening skies,
Perchance we may,
Where now this night is day,
And even through faith of still averted feet,
Making full circle of our banishment,
Amazed meet;
The bitter journey to the bourne so sweet
Seasoning the termless feast of our content
With tears of recognition never dry.

from *To the Unknown Eros*

Popular Song

My gal's a out-and-outer,
That is she's not a muff,
There's no two ways about her,
She's a proper bit of stuff.
When on Sunday dress'd all in her best,
She's flash but she's discreet,
She's as straight as any sausage,
And a dozen times more sweet.

Oh, you ought to see my Sarah,
She's a spiffin bit of stuff,
You'll never find a fairer,
She's nature in the rough,
She's never out of collar,
So excuse me if I holler –
Whoe, – ain't I nuts on
Blooming little Sarah.

Anon

Popular Pastoral

As I walked out one morning I met a buxom lass,
Belonging to a dairy man, she had a field of grass,
It grew between two mountains at the foot of a rising hill,
She bir'd me to cut it down while the birds did sweetly sing.

She said, my lusty young man, will you now begin,
My grass is in good order, I long to have it down,
It is such pleasant weather I long to clear the ground,
So get your scythe in order to mow my meadow down.

Anon

CHRISTINA ROSSETTI

Remember

Remember me when I am gone away,
   Gone far away into the silent land;
   When you can no more hold me by the hand.
Nor I half turn to go yet turning stay.
Remember me when no more day by day
   You tell me of our future that you plann'd:
   Only remember me; you understand
It will be late to counsel then or pray.
Yet if you should forget me for a while
   And afterwards remember, do not grieve:
   For if the darkness and corruption leave
   A vestige of the thoughts that once I had,
Better by far you should forget and smile
   Than that you should remember and be sad.

A Birthday

My heart is like a singing bird
   Whose nest is in a watered shoot:
My heart is like an apple-tree
   Whose boughs are bent with thickset fruit;
My heart is like a rainbow shell
   That paddles in a halcyon sea;
My heart is gladder than all these
   Because my love is come to me.

Raise me a dais of silk and down;
   Hang it with vair and purple dyes;
Carve it in doves and pomegranates,
   And peacocks with a hundred eyes;
Work it in gold and silver grapes,
   In leaves and silver fleurs-de-lys;
Because the birthday of my life
   Is come, my love is come to me.

Song

When I am dead, my dearest,
   Sing no sad songs for me;
Plant thou no roses at my head,
   Nor shady cypress tree:
Be the green grass above me
   With showers and dewdrops wet:
And if thou wilt, remember,
   And if thou wilt, forget.

I shall not see the shadows,
   I shall not feel the rain;
I shall not hear the nightingale
   Sing on as if in pain:
And dreaming through the twilight
   That doth not rise nor set,
Haply I may remember,
   And haply may forget.

Echo

Come to me the silence of the night;
  Come in the speaking silence of a dream;
Come with soft rounded cheeks and eyes as bright
    As sunlight on a stream;
      Come back in tears,
O memory, hope, love of finished years.

O dream how sweet, too sweet, too bitter sweet,
  Whose wakening should have been in Paradise,
Where souls brimfull of love abide and meet;
    Where thirsting longing eyes
      Watch the slow door
That opening, letting in, lets out no more.

Yet come to me in dreams, that I may live
  My very life again though cold in death:
Come back to me in dreams, that I may give
    Pulse for pulse, breath for breath:
      Speak low, lean low,
As long ago, my love, how long ago.

Dante Gabriel Rossetti

from *Jenny*

'Vengeance of Jenny's case! Fie on her! Never name her, child!' *Mrs Quickly*

Lazy laughing languid Jenny,
Fond of a kiss and fond of a guinea,
Whose head upon my knee to-night
Rests for a while, as if grown light
With all our dances and the sound
To which the wild tunes spun you round:
Fair Jenny mine, the thoughtless queen
Of kisses which the blush between
Could hardly make much daintier;
Whose eyes are as blue skies, whose hair
Is countless gold incomparable:
Fresh flower, scarce touched with signs that tell
Of Love's exuberant hotbed: – Nay,
Poor flower left torn since yesterday
Until to-morrow leave you bare;
Poor handful of bright spring-water
Flung in the whirlpool's shrieking face;
Poor shameful Jenny, full of grace
Thus with your head upon my knee; –
Whose person or whose purse may be
The lodestar of your reverie?

DANTE GABRIEL ROSSETTI

Sudden Light

I have been here before,
　But when or how I cannot tell:
I know the grass beyond the door,
　The sweet keen smell,
The sighing sound, the lights around the shore.

You have been mine before, –
　How long ago I may not know:
But just when at the swallow's soar
　Your neck turned so,
Some veil did fall, – I knew it all of yore.

Then, now, – perchance again! . . . .
　O round mine eyes your tresses shake!
Shall we not lie as we have lain
　Thus for Love's sake,
And sleep, and wake, yet never break the chain?

Ballata

Of a continual Death in Love

Though thou, indeed, hast quite forgotten ruth,
Its steadfast truth my heart abandons not;
But still its thought yields service in good part
　To that hard heart in thee.

Alas! who hears believes not I am so.
Yet who can know? of very surety, none.
From Love is won a spirit, in some wise,
　Which dies perpetually:

And, when at length in that strange ecstasy
   The heavy sigh will start,
   There rains upon my heart
   A love so pure and fine,
That I say: 'Lady, I am wholly thine.'

after Guido Cavalcanti

Bernardo da Bologna
to Guido Cavalcanti

He writes to Guido, telling him of the Love
which a certain Pinella showed on seeing him

Unto that lowly lovely maid, I wis,
   So poignant in the heart was thy salute,
   That she changed countenance, remaining mute.
Wherefore I asked: 'Pinella, how is this?
Hast heard of Guido? know'st thou who he is?'
   She answered, 'Yea;' then paused, irresolute;
   But I saw well how the love-wounds acute
Were widened, and the star which Love calls his
Filled her with gentle brightness perfectly.
   'But, friend, an't please thee, I would have it told,'
She said, 'how I am known to him through thee.
   Yet since, scarce seen, I knew his name of old, –
Even as the riddle is read, so must it be.
   Oh! send him love of mine a thousand-fold!'

after Guido Cavalcanti

To Bernardo da Bologna

*Guido answers, commending Pinella, and saying that the Love
he can offer her is already shared by many noble Ladies*

The fountain-head that is so bright to see
    Gains as it runs in virtue and in sheen,
Friend Bernard; and for her who spoke with thee,
    Even such the flow of her young life has been:
So that when Love discourses secretly
    Of things the fairest he has ever seen,
He says there is no fairer thing than she,
    A lowly maid as lovely as a queen.
And for that I am troubled, thinking of
    That sigh wherein I burn upon the waves
      Which drift her heart, – poor barque, so ill bested! –
Unto Pinella a great river of love
    I send, that's full of sirens, and whose slaves
      Are beautiful and richly habited.

after Guido Cavalcanti

Ballata

In Exile at Sarzana

Because I think not ever to return,
    Ballad, to Tuscany, –
Go therefore thou for me
    Straight to my lady's face,
    Who, of her noble grace,
Shall show thee courtesy.

Thou seekest her in charge of many sighs,
    Full of much grief and of exceeding fear.
But have good heed thou come not to the eyes
    Of such as are sworn foes to gentle cheer:
    For, certes, if this thing should chance, – from her
        Thou then couldst only look
        For scorn, and such rebuke
        As needs must bring me pain; –
        Yea, after death again
        Tears and fresh agony.

Surely thou knowest, Ballad, how that Death
    Assails me, till my life is almost sped:
Thou knowest how my heart still travaileth
    Through the sore pangs which in my soul are bred: ·
    My body being now so nearly dead,
        It cannot suffer more.
        Then, going, I implore
        That this my soul thou take
        (Nay, do so for my sake,)
        When my heart sets it free.

Ah! Ballad, unto thy dear offices
    I do commend my soul, thus trembling;
That thou mayst lead it, for pure piteousness,
    Even to that lady's presence whom I sing.
    Ah! Ballad, say thou to her, sorrowing,
        Whereso thou meet her then: –
        'This thy poor handmaiden
        Is come, nor will be gone,
        Being parted now from one
        Who served Love painfully.'

Thou also, thou bewildered voice and weak,
    That goest forth in tears from my grieved heart,
Shalt, with my soul and with this ballad, speak
    Of my dead mind, when thou dost hence depart,
Unto that lady (piteous as thou art!)
      Who is so calm and bright,
      It shall be deep delight
      To feel her presence there.
      And thou, Soul, worship her
      Still in her purity.

after Guido Cavalcanti

ALGERNON CHARLES SWINBURNE

from *Anactoria*

Anactoria was one of the young women whom the poetess Sappho loved.

Ah that my lips were tuneless lips, but pressed
To the bruised blossom of thy scourged white breast!
Ah that my mouth for Muses' milk were fed
On the sweet blood thy sweet small wounds had bled!
That with my tongue I felt them, and could taste
The faint flakes from thy bosom to the waist!
That I could drink thy veins as wine, and eat
Thy breasts like honey! that from face to feet
Thy body were abolished and consumed,
And in my flesh thy very flesh entombed!
Ah, ah, thy beauty! like a beast it bites,
Stings like an adder, like an arrow smites.
Ah sweet, and sweet again, and seven times sweet,
The paces and the pauses of thy feet!
Ah sweeter than all sleep or summer air
The fallen fillets fragrant from thine hair!
Yea, though their alien kisses do me wrong,
Sweeter thy lips than mine with all their song;

Thy shoulders whiter than a fleece of white,
And flower-sweet fingers, good to bruise or bite
As honeycomb of the inmost honey-cells,
With almond-shaped and roseleaf-coloured shells
And blood like purple blossom at the tips
Quivering; and pain made perfect in thy lips
For my sake when I hurt thee; O that I
Durst crush thee out of life with love, and die,
Die of thy pain and my delight, and be
Mixed with thy blood and molten into thee!

The Sundew

A little marsh-plant, yellow green
And pricked at lip with tender red.
Tread close, and either way you tread
Some faint black water jets between
Lest you should bruise the curious head.

A live thing maybe; who shall know?
The summer knows and suffers it;
For the cool moss is thick and sweet
Each side, and saves the blossom so
That it lives out the long June heat.

The deep scent of the heather burns
About it; breathless though it be,
Bow down and worship; more than we
Is the least flower whose life returns,
Least weed renascent in the sea.

We are vexed and cumbered in earth's sight
With wants, with many memories;
These see their mother what she is,
Glad-growing, till August leave more bright
The apple-coloured cranberries.

Wind blows and bleaches the strong grass,
Blown all one way to shelter it
From trample of strayed kine, with feet
Felt heavier than the moorhen was,
Strayed up past patches of wild wheat.

You call it sundew: how it grows,
If with its colour it have breath,
If life taste sweet to it, if death
Pain its soft petal, no man knows:
Man has no sight or sense that saith.

My sundew, grown of gentle days,
In these green miles the spring begun
Thy growth ere April had half done
With the soft secret of her ways
Or June made ready for the sun.

O red-lipped mouth of marsh-flower,
I have a secret halved with thee.
The name that is love's name to me
Thou knowest, and the face of her
Who is my festival to see.

The hard sun, as thy petals knew,
Coloured the heavy moss-water:
Thou wert not worth green midsummer
Nor fit to live to August blue,
O sundew, not remembering her.

ALGERNON CHARLES SWINBURNE

Satia Te Sanguine

If you loved me ever so little,
   I could bear the bonds that gall,
I could dream the bonds were brittle;
   You do not love me at all.

O beautiful lips, O bosom
   More white than the moon's and warm,
A sterile, a ruinous blossom
   Is blown your way in a storm.

As the lost white feverish limbs
   Of the Lesbian Sappho, adrift
In foam where the sea-weed swims,
   Swam loose for the streams to lift,

My heart swims blind in a sea
   That stuns me; swims to and fro,
And gathers to windward and lee
   Lamentation, and mourning, and woe.

A broken, an emptied boat,
   Sea saps it, winds blow apart,
Sick and adrift and afloat,
   The barren waif of a heart.

Where, when the gods would be cruel,
   Do they go for a torture? where
Plant thorns, set pain like a jewel?
   Ah, not in the flesh, not there!

The racks of earth and the rods
    Are weak as foam on the sands;
In the heart is the prey for gods,
    Who crucify hearts, not hands.

Mere pangs corrode and consume,
    Dead when life dies in the brain;
In the infinite spirit is room
    For the pulse of an infinite pain.

I wish you were dead, my dear;
    I would give you, had I to give,
Some death too bitter to fear;
    It is better to die than live.

I wish you were stricken of thunder
    And burnt with a bright flame through,
Consumed and cloven in sunder,
    I dead at your feet like you.

If I could but know after all,
    I might cease to hunger and ache,
Though your heart were ever so small,
    If it were not a stone or a snake.

You are crueller, you that we love,
    Than hatred, hunger, or death;
You have eyes and breasts like a dove,
    And you kill men's hearts with a breath.

As plague in a poisonous city
    Insults and exults on her dead,
So you, when pallid for pity
    Comes love, and fawns to be fed.

As a tame beast writhes and wheedles,
  He fawns to be fed with wiles;
You carve him a cross of needles,
  And whet them sharp as your smiles.

He is patient of thorn and whip,
  He is dumb under axe or dart;
You suck with a sleepy red lip
  The wet red wounds in his heart.

You thrill as his pulses dwindle,
  You brighten and warm as he bleeds,
With insatiable eyes that kindle
  And insatiable mouth that feeds.

Your hands nailed love to the tree,
  You stript him, scourged him with rods,
And drowned him deep in the sea
  That hides the dead and their gods.

And for all this, die will he not;
  There is no man sees him but I;
You came and went and forgot;
  I hope he will some day die.

A Match

If love were what the rose is,
  And I were like the leaf,
Our lives would grow together
In sad or singing weather,
Blown fields or flowerful closes,
  Green pleasure or grey grief;
If love were what the rose is,
  And I were like the leaf.

If I were what the words are,
    And love were like the tune,
With double sound and single
Delight our lips would mingle,
With kisses glad as birds are
    That get sweet rain at noon;
If I were what the words are,
    And love were like the tune.

If you were life, my darling,
    And I your love were death,
We'd shine and snow together
Ere March made sweet the weather
With daffodil and starling
    And hours of fruitful breath;
If you were life, my darling,
    And I your love were death.

If you were thrall to sorrow,
    And I were page to joy,
We'd play for lives and seasons
With loving looks and treasons
And tears of night and morrow
    And laughs of maid and boy;
If you were thrall to sorrow,
    And I were page to joy.

If you were April's lady,
    And I were lord in May,
We'd throw with leaves for hours
And draw for days with flowers,
Till day like night were shady
    And night were bright like day;
If you were April's lady,
    And I were lord in May.

If you were queen of pleasure,
   And I were king to pain,
We'd hunt down love together,
Pluck out his flying-feather,
And teach his feet a measure,
   And find his mouth a rein;
If you were queen of pleasure,
   And I were king of pain.

ARTHUR SYMONS

Under the Cliffs

Bright light to windward on the horizon's verge;
To leeward, stormy shadows, violet-black,
And the wide sea between
A vast unfurrowed field of windless green;
The stormy shadows flicker on the track
Of phantom sails that vanish and emerge.

I gaze across the sea, remembering her;
I watch the white sun walk across the sea,
This pallid afternoon,
With feet that tread as whitely as the moon,
And in his fleet and shining feet I see
The footsteps of another voyager.

Pastel

The light of our cigarettes
Went and came in the gloom:
It was dark in the little room.

Dark, and then, in the dark,
Sudden, a flash, a glow,
And a hand and a ring I know.

And then, through the dark, a flush
Ruddy and vague, the grace
(A rose!) of her lyric face.

ARTHUR SYMONS

White Heliotrope

The feverish room and that white bed,
The tumbled skirts upon a chair,
The novel flung half-open, where
Hat, hair-pins, puffs, and paints, are spread;

The mirror that has sucked your face
Into its secret deep of deeps,
And there mysteriously keeps
Forgotten memories of grace;

And you, half dressed and half awake,
Your slant eyes strangely watching me,
And I, who watch you drowsily,
With eyes that, having slept not, ache;

This (need one dread? nay, dare one hope?)
Will rise, a ghost of memory, if
Ever again my handkerchief
Is scented with White Heliotrope.

LORD DE TABLEY

Sonnet

Rosy delight that changest day by day
From dearest growing to a dearer favour,
Whom Thought and Sinew bondsmen to obey,
Slave out thy least command and may not waver.

My recompense and zenith of reward
Bourn of all effort, thought behind all thinking,
Regent of sleep and centre of regard
Whereon the wakeful soul will pore unshrinking.

I cannot count the phases of this love,
Measure its growth or vindicate its reason.
I cannot doubt; the very smile that wove
My soul with love withholds me from love's treason.

I only know thou art my best delight,
Food of sweet thoughts and sum of all things bright.

Sonnet

I look'd across the river for the morn.
The clouds came not, the air was very slow,
Till on the region past an underglow
And scorch'd the glimmering mantle of the dawn.

The one clear star set in a branch of rose
Drew in before the river of bold light,
Foiling the ragged clouds to left and right,
To sort a crystal lake of raying glows.

I could not rest; a wilderness of mind
Was strong within me; love and shame and thought
Of days behind, at one instant caught
To reason from the mental store-house blind.

Last thou, fair lily head, beyond night's fall
Stepp'd in warm sleep, sweet central wish of all!

Mutation

If but a little while the flowers are new
Till broken over-ripely with great dew,
Shall Love remain untarnished till his close,
Clear in his depth, heart-perfect like a rose?

Yet, O my love, one little changeful year
O'er Amor's laughing eyes will render sere
The pretty petals, and uncrimson soon
The brave new posies garlanded in June.

If I have led thee in sweet way of flowers,
If we have heard the dove's voice answer ours,
Where the sharp woods grew mellow nearer noon,
Shall love endure more than the cuckoo's tune?

If I have pastured at thy lips as well
As the bee trembles at the asphodel,
Are their ripe bloom and tender incense breath
Secure alone from stain of dust and death?

Love in his sheaf has bound us breast to breast,
Why reason sourly at his harvest feast:
Or seek for ashes under every rose
That cinctures round his beaming tresses close?

And yet, dear heart, this phantom clothed in fear,
Makes not in dearness thee one shade less dear;
And I will hunger for more love indeed,
If love be briefer than a wayside weed.

I will not leave my ruler, tho' his reign
Change as a rose or like a crescent wane.
What answer shall we render, sweet, to these
Who hate our Lord, because his rule shall cease?

Say, with thy sweet lip rested under mine,
'Lord of an hour, thou only art divine'.
Sing, while I feel the perfume of thy breath,
'Love is eternal and more strong than death.'

Nuptial Song

'Sigh, heart, break not'

Sigh, heart, and break not; rest, lark, and wake not!
    Day I hear coming to draw my Love away.
As mere-waves whisper, and clouds grow crisper,
    Ah, like a rose he will waken up with day.

In moon-light lonely, he is my Love only,
    I share with none when Luna rides in grey.
As dawn-beams quicken, my rivals thicken,
    The light and deed and turmoil of the day.

To watch my sleeper to me is sweeter,
    Than any waking words my love can say:
In dream he finds me and closer winds me!
    Let him rest by me a little more and stay.

Ah, mine eyes, close not: and, tho' he knows not,
    My lips, on his be tender while you may;
Ere leaves are shaken, and ring-doves waken,
    And infant buds begin to scent new day.

Fair Darkness, measure thine hours, as treasure
    Shed each one slowly from thine urn, I pray;
Hoard in and cover each from my lover;
    I cannot lose him yet; dear night, delay.

Each moment dearer, true-love, lie nearer,
    My hair shall blind thee lest thou see the ray;
My locks encumber thine ears in slumber,
    Lest any bird dare give thee note of day.

He rests so calmly; we lie so warmly;
    Hand within hand, as children after play; –
In shafted amber on roof and chamber
    Dawn enters; my Love wakens; here is day.

A Leave-Taking

Kneel not and leave me: mirth is in its grave.
    True friend, sweet words were ours, sweet words decay.
Believe, the perfume once this violet gave
    Lives – lives no more, though mute tears answer nay.
        Break off delay!

Dead, Love is dead! Ay, cancelled all his due.
    We say he mocks repose – we cannot tell –
Close up his eyes and crown his head with rue,
    Say in his ear, sweet Love, farewell! farewell!
        A last low knell.

Forbear to move him. Peace, why should we stay?
    Go back no more to listen for his tread.
Resume our old calm face of every day:
    Not all our kneeling turns that sacred head
        Long dear, long dead!

Go with no tear-drop; Love had died before:
    Stay being foolish; being wise begone.
Let severed ways estrange thy weak heart more.
    Go, unregretfull, and refrain thy moan.
        Depart alone.

ALFRED, LORD TENNYSON

Mariana

'Mariana in the moated grange.' *Measure for Measure.*

With blackest moss the flower-plots
    Were thickly crusted, one and all:
The rusted nails fell from the knots
    That held the pear to the gable-wall.
The broken sheds look'd sad and strange:
    Unlifted was the clinking latch;
    Weeded and worn the ancient thatch
Upon the lonely moated grange.
        She only said, 'My life is dreary,
            He cometh not,' she said;
        She said, 'I am aweary, aweary,
            I would that I were dead!'

Her tears fell with the dews at even;
    Her tears fell ere the dews were dried;
She could not look on the sweet heaven,
    Either at morn or eventide.
After the flitting of the bats,
    When thickest dark did trance the sky,
    She drew her casement-curtain by,
And glanced athwart the glooming flats.
        She only said, 'The night is dreary,
            He cometh not,' she said;
        She said, 'I am aweary, aweary,
            I would that I were dead!'

Upon the middle of the night,
   Waking she heard the night-fowl crow:
The cock sung out an hour ere light:
   From the dark fen the oxen's low
Came to her: without hope of change,
   In sleep she seem'd to walk forlorn,
   Till cold winds woke the gray-eyed morn
About the lonely moated grange.
      She only said, 'The day is dreary,
        He cometh not,' she said;
      She said, 'I am aweary, aweary,
        I would that I were dead!'

About a stone-cast from the wall
   A sluice with blacken'd water slept,
And o'er it many, round and small,
   The cluster'd marish-mosses crept.
Hard by a poplar shook alway,
   All silver-green with gnarled bark:
   For leagues no other tree did mark
The level waste, the rounding gray.
      She only said, 'My life is dreary,
        He cometh not,' she said;
      She said, 'I am aweary, aweary,
        I would that I were dead!'

And ever when the moon was low,
    And the shrill winds were up and away,
In the white curtain, to and fro,
    She saw the gusty shadow sway.
But when the moon was very low,
    And wild winds bound within their cell,
    The shadow of the poplar fell
Upon her bed, across her brow.
        She only said, 'The night is dreary,
           He cometh not,' she said;
        She said, 'I am aweary, aweary,
           I would that I were dead!'

All day within the dreamy house,
    The doors upon their hinges creak'd;
The blue fly sung in the pane; the mouse
    Behind the mouldering wainscot shriek'd,
Or from the crevice peer'd about.
    Old faces glimmer'd thro' the doors,
    Old footsteps trod the upper floors,
Old voices called her from without.
        She only said, 'My life is dreary,
           He cometh not,' she said;
        She said, 'I am aweary, aweary,
           I would that I were dead!'

The sparrow's chirrup on the roof,
   The slow clock ticking, and the sound
Which to the wooing wind aloof
   The poplar made, did all confound
Her sense; but most she loathed the hour
   When the thick-moted sunbeam lay
   Athwart the chambers, and the day
Was sloping toward his western bower,
     Then, said she, 'I am very dreary,
      He will not come,' she said;
     She wept, 'I am aweary, aweary,
      Oh God, that I were dead!'

from *The Princess*

'O Swallow, Swallow, flying, flying South,
Fly to her, and fall upon her gilded eaves,
And tell her, tell her, what I tell to thee.

'O tell her, Swallow, thou that knowest each,
That bright and fierce and fickle is the South,
And dark and true and tender is the North.

'O Swallow, Swallow, if I could follow, and light
Upon her lattice, I would pipe and trill,
And cheep and twitter twenty million loves.

'O were I thou that she might take me in,
And lay me on her bosom, and her heart
Would rock the snowy cradle till I died.

'Why lingereth she to clothe her heart with love,
Delaying as the tender ash delays
To clothe herself, when all the woods are green?

'O tell her, Swallow, that thy brood is flown:
Say to her, I do but wanton in the South,
But in the North long since my nest is made.

'O tell her, brief is life but love is long,
And brief the sun of summer in the North,
And brief the moon of beauty in the South.

'O Swallow, flying from the golden woods,
Fly to her, and pipe and woo her, and make her mine,
And tell her, tell her, that I follow thee.'

* * *

Ask me no more: the moon may draw the sea;
    The cloud may stoop from heaven and take the shape
      With fold to fold, of mountain or of cape;
But O too fond, when have I answer'd thee?
                    Ask me no more.

Ask me no more: what answer should I give?
    I love not hollow cheek or faded eye:
      Yet, O my friend, I will not have thee die!
Ask me no more, lest I should bid thee live;
                    Ask me no more.

Ask me no more: thy fate and mine are seal'd:
    I strove against the stream and all in vain:
      Let the great river take me to the main:
No more, dear love, for at a touch I yield;
                    Ask me no more.

* * *

'Now sleeps the crimson petal, now the white;
Nor waves the cypress in the palace walk;
Nor winks the gold fin in the porphyry font:
The fire-fly wakens: waken thou with me.

Now droops the milkwhite peacock like a ghost,
And like a ghost she glimmers on to me.

Now lies the Earth all Danaë to the stars,
And all thy heart lies open unto me.

Now slides the silent meteor on, and leaves
A shining furrow, as thy thoughts in me.

Now folds the lily all her sweetness up,
And slips into the bosom of the lake:
So fold thyself, my dearest, thou, and slip
Into my bosom and be lost in me.'

* * *

'Come down, O maid, from yonder mountain height:
What pleasure lives in height (the shepherd sang)
In height and cold, the splendour of the hills?
But cease to move so near the Heavens, and cease
To glide a sunbeam by the blasted Pine,
To sit a star upon the sparkling spire;
And come, for Love is of the valley, come,
For Love is of the valley, come thou down
And find him; by the happy threshold, he,
Or hand in hand with Plenty in the maize,
Or red with spirted purple of the vats,
Or foxlike in the vine; nor cares to walk
With Death and Morning on the silver horns,
Nor wilt thou snare him in the white ravine,
Nor find him dropt upon the firths of ice,
That huddling slant in furrow-cloven falls
To roll the torrent out of dusky doors:
But follow; let the torrent dance thee down
To find him in the valley; let the wild
Lean-headed Eagles yelp alone, and leave
The monstrous ledges there to slope, and spill
Their thousand wreaths of dangling water-smoke,
That like a broken purpose waste in air:
So waste not thou; but come; for all the vales
Await thee; azure pillars of the hearth
Arise to thee; the children call, and I
Thy shepherd pipe, and sweet is every sound,
Sweeter thy voice , but every sound is sweet;
Myriads of rivulets hurrying thro' the lawn,
The moan of doves in immemorial elms,
And murmuring of innumerable bees.'

ALFRED, LORD TENNYSON

from *In Memoriam A.H.H.*

In Memoriam was published in 1850. In it the poet expresses his
grief for the loss of his friend, Arthur Hallam, whom he had met
at Cambridge and who had died in 1833.

Dark house, by which once more I stand
　　Here in the long unlovely street,
　　Doors, where my heart was used to beat
So quickly, waiting for a hand,

A hand that can be clasp'd no more –
　　Behold me, for I cannot sleep,
　　And like a guilty thing I creep
At earliest morning to the door.

He is not here; but far away
　　The noise of life begins again,
　　And ghastly thro' the drizzling rain
On the bald street breaks the blank day.

* * *

I cannot love thee as I ought,
　　For love reflects the thing beloved;
　　My words are only words, and moved
Upon the topmost froth of thought.

'Yet blame not thou thy plaintive song,'
　　The Spirit of true love replied;
　　'Thou canst not move me from thy side,
Nor human frailty do me wrong.

'What keeps a spirit wholly true
 To that ideal which he bears?
 What record? not the sinless years
That breathed beneath the Syrian blue:

'So fret not, like an idle girl,
 That life is dash'd with flecks of sin.
 Abide: thy wealth is gather'd in,
When Time hath sunder'd shell from pearl.'

* * *

Could I have said while he was here,
 'My love shall now no further range;
 There cannot come a mellower change,
For now is love mature in ear'!

Love, then, had hope of richer store:
 What end is here to my complaint?
 This haunting whisper makes me faint,
'More years had made me love thee more.'

But Death returns an answer sweet:
 'My sudden frost was sudden gain,
 And gave all ripeness to the grain,
It might have drawn from after-heat.'

* * *

I wage not any feud with Death
    For changes wrought on form and face;
    No lower life that earth's embrace
May breed with him, can fright my faith.

Eternal process moving on,
    From state to state the spirit walks;
    And these are but the shatter'd stalks,
Or ruin'd chrysalis of one.

Nor blame I Death, because he bare
    The use of virtue out of earth:
    I know transplanted human worth
Will bloom to profit, otherwhere.

For this alone on Death I wreak
    The wrath that garners in my heart;
    He put our lives so far apart
We cannot hear each other speak.

* * *

I woo your love: I count it crime
   To mourn for any overmuch;
   I, the divided half of such
A friendship as had master'd Time;

Which masters Time indeed, and is
   Eternal, separate from fears:
   The all-assuming months and years
Can take no part away from this:

But Summer on the steaming floods,
   And Spring that swells the narrow brooks,
   And Autumn, with a noise of rooks,
That gather in the waning woods,

And every pulse of wind and wave
   Recalls, in change of light or gloom,
   My old affection of the tomb,
And my prime passion in the grave:

My old affection of the tomb,
   A part of stillness yearns to speak:
   'Arise and get thee forth and seek
A friendship for the years to come.

'I watch thee from the quiet shore;
   Thy spirit up to mine can reach;
   But in dear words of human speech
We two communicate no more.'

And I, 'Can clouds of nature stain
   The starry clearness of the free?
   How is it? Canst thou feel for me
Some painless sympathy with pain?'

And lightly does the whisper fall;
 ''Tis hard for thee to fathom this;
 I triumph in conclusive bliss,
And that serene result of all.'

So hold I commerce with the dead;
 Or so methinks the dead would say;
 Or so shall grief with symbols play
And pining life be fancy-fed.

Now looking to some settled end,
 That these things pass, and I shall prove
 A meeting somewhere, love with love,
I crave your pardon, O my friend;

If not so fresh, with love as true,
 I, clasping brother-hands, aver
 I could not, if I would, transfer
The whole I felt for him to you.

For which be they that hold apart
 The promise of the golden hours?
 First love, first friendship, equal powers,
That marry with the virgin heart.

Still mine, that cannot but deplore,
 That beats within a lonely place,
 That yet remembers his embrace,
But at his footstep leaps no more,

My heart, tho' widow'd, may not rest
 Quite in the love of what is gone,
 But seeks to beat in time with one
That warms another living breast.

Ah, take the imperfect gift I bring,
    Knowing the primrose yet is dear,
    The primrose of the later year,
As not unlike to that of Spring.

* * *

By night we linger'd on the lawn,
    For underfoot the herb was dry;
    And genial warmth; and o'er the sky
The silvery haze of summer drawn;

And calm that let the tapers burn
    Unwavering: not a cricket chirr'd:
    The brook alone far-off was heard
And on the board the fluttering urn:

And bats went round in fragrant skies,
    And wheel'd or lit the filmy shapes
    That haunt the dusk, with ermine capes
And woolly breasts and beaded eyes;

While now we sang old songs that peal'd
    From knoll to knoll, where couch'd at ease,
    The white kine glimmer'd, and the trees
Laid their dark arms about the field.

But when those others, one by one,
    Withdrew themselves from me and night,
    And in the house light after light
Went out, and I was all alone,

A hunger seized my heart; I read
    Of that glad year which once had been,
    In those fall'n leaves which kept their green,
The noble letters of the dead:

And strangely on the silence broke
    The silent-speaking words, and strange
    Was love's dumb cry defying change
To test his worth; and strangely spoke

The faith, the vigour, bold to dwell
    On doubts that drive the coward back,
    And keen thro' wordly snares to track
Suggestion to her inmost cell.

So word by word, and line by line
    The dead man touch'd me from the past,
    And all at once it seem'd at last
The living soul was flash'd on mine,

And mine in this was wound, and whirl'd
    About empyreal heights of thought,
    And came on that which is, and caught
The deep pulsations of the world,

Æonian music measuring out
    The steps of Time – the shocks of Chance –
    The blows of Death. At length my trace
Was cancell'd, stricken thro' with doubt.

Vague words! but ah, how hard to frame
    In matter-moulded forms of speech,
    Or ev'n for intellect to reach
Thro' memory that which I became:

Till now the doubtful dusk reveal'd
    The knolls once more where, couch'd at ease,
    The white kine glimmer'd, and the trees
Laid their dark arms about the field:

And suck'd from out the distant gloom
   A breeze began to tremble o'er
   The large leaves of the sycamore,
And fluctuate all the still perfume,

And gathering freshlier overhead,
   Rock'd the full-foliaged elms, and swung
   The heavy-folded rose, and flung
The lilies to and fro, and said

'The dawn, the dawn,' and died away;
   And East and West, without a breath,
   Mixt their dim lights, like life and death,
To broaden into boundless day.

* * *

My love has talk'd with rocks and trees;
   He finds on misty mountain-ground
   His own vast shadow glory-crown'd;
He sees himself in all he sees.

Two partners of a married life –
   I look'd on these and thought of thee
   In vastness and in mystery,
And of my spirit as of a wife.

These two – they dwelt with eye on eye,
   Their hearts of old have beat in tune,
   Their meetings made December June,
Their every parting was to die.

Their love has never past away;
   The days she never can forget
   And earnest that he loves her yet,
Whate'er the faithless people say.

Her life is lone, he sits apart,
    He loves her yet, she will not weep,
    Tho' rapt in matters dark and deep
He seems to slight her simple heart.

He thrids the labyrinth of the mind,
    He reads the secret of the star,
    He seems so near and yet so far,
He looks so cold: she thinks him kind.

She keeps the gift of years before,
    A wither'd violet is her bliss:
    She knows not what his greatness is,
For that, for all, she loves him more

For him she plays, to him she sings
    Of early faith and plighted vows;
    She knows but matters of the house,
And he, he knows a thousand things.

Her faith is fixt and cannot move,
    She darkly feels him great and wise,
    She dwells on him with faithful eyes,
'I cannot understand: I love.'

* * *

Doors, where my heart was used to beat
   So quickly, not as one that weeps
   I come once more; the city sleeps;
I smell the meadow in the street;

I hear a chirp of birds; I see
   Betwixt the black fronts long-withdrawn
   A light-blue lane of early dawn,
And think of early days and thee,

And bless thee, for thy lips are bland,
   And bright the friendship of thine eye;
   And in my thoughts with scarce a sigh
I take the pressure of thine hand.

ALFRED, LORD TENNYSON

from *Maud: A Monodrama*

FROM PART I

I have led her home, my love, my only friend.
There is none like her, none.
And never yet so warmly ran my blood
And sweetly, on and on
Calming itself to the long-wish'd-for end,
Full to the banks, close on the promised good.

None like her, none.
Just now the dry-tongued laurels' pattering talk
Seem'd her light foot along the garden walk,
And shook my heart to think she comes once more;
But even then I heard her close the door,
The gates of Heaven are closed, and she is gone.

There is none like her, none.
Nor will be when our summers have deceased.
O, art thou sighing for Lebanon
In the long breeze that streams to thy delicious East,
Sighing for Lebanon,
Dark cedar, tho' thy limbs have here increased,
Upon a pastoral slope as fair,
And looking to the South, and fed
With honey'd rain and delicate air,
And haunted by the starry head
Of her whose gentle will has changed my fate,
And made my life a perfumed altar-flame;
And over whom thy darkness must have spread
With such delight as theirs of old, thy great
Forefathers of the thornless garden, there
Shadowing the snow-limb'd Eve from whom she came.

Here will I lie, while these long branches sway,
And you fair stars that crown a happy day
Go in and out as if at merry play,
Who am no more so all forlorn,
As when it seem'd far better to be born
To labour and the mattock-harden'd hand,
Than nursed at ease and brought to understand
A sad astrology, the boundless plan
That makes you tyrants in your iron skies,
Innumerable, pitiless, passionless eyes,
Cold fires, yet with power to burn and brand
His nothingness into man.

But now shine on, and what care I,
Who in this stormy gulf have found a pearl
The countercharm of space and hollow sky,
And do accept my madness, and would die
To save from some light shame one simple girl.

Would die; for sullen-seeming Death may give
More life to Love than is or ever was
In our low world, where yet 'tis sweet to live.
Let no one ask me how it came to pass;
It seems that I am happy, that to me
A livelier emerald twinkles in the grass,
A purer sapphire melts into the sea.

Not die; but live a life of truest breath,
And teach true life to fight with mortal wrongs.
O, why should Love, like men in drinking-songs,
Spice his fair banquet with the dust of death?
Make answer, Maud my bliss,
Maud made my Maud by that long loving kiss,
Life of my life, wilt thou not answer this?
'The dusky strand of Death inwoven here
With dear Love's tie, makes Love himself more dear.'

Is that enchanted moan only the swell
Of the long waves that roll in yonder bay?
And hark the clock within, the silver knell
Of twelve sweet hours that past in bridal white
And died to live, long as my pulses play:
But now by this my love has closed her sight
And given false death her hand, and stol'n away
To dreamful wastes where footless fancies dwell
Among the fragments of the golden day.
May nothing there her maiden grace affright!
Dear heart, I feel with thee the drowsy spell.
My bride to be, my evermore delight,
My own heart's heart, my ownest own, farewell;
It is but for a little space I go:
And ye meanwhile far over moor and fell
Beat to the noiseless music of the night!
Has our whole earth gone nearer to the glow
Of your soft splendours that you look so bright?
I have climb'd nearer out of lonely Hell.
Beat, happy stars, timing with things below,
Beat with my heart more blest than heart can tell,
Blest, but for some dark undercurrent woe
That seems to draw – but it shall not be so:
Let all be well, be well.

* * *

Come into the garden, Maud,
    For the black bat, night, has flown,
Come into the garden, Maud,
    I am here at the gate alone;
And the woodbine spices are wafted abroad,
    And the musk of the rose is blown.

For a breeze of morning moves,
 And the planet of Love is on high,
Beginning to faint in the light that she loves
 On a bed of daffodil sky,
To faint in the light of the sun she loves,
 To faint in his light, and to die.

All night have the roses heard
 The flute, violin, bassoon;
All night has the casement jessamine stirr'd
 To the dancers dancing in tune;
Till a silence fell with the waking bird,
 And a hush with the setting moon.

I said to the lily, 'There is but one
 With whom she has heart to be gay.
When will the dancers leave her alone?
 She is weary of dance and play.'
Now half to the setting moon are gone,
 And half to the rising day;
Low on the sand and loud on the stone
 The last wheel echoes away.

I said to the rose, 'The brief night goes
 In babble and revel and wine.
O young lord-lover, what sighs are those,
 For one that will never be thine?
But mine, but mine,' so I sware to the rose,
 'For ever and ever, mine.'

And the soul of the rose went into my blood,
 As the music clash'd in the hall;
And long by the garden lake I stood,
 For I heard your rivulet fall
From the lake to the meadow and on to the wood,
 Our wood, that is dearer than all;

From the meadow your walks have left so sweet
    That whenever a March-wind sighs
He sets the jewel-print of your feet
    In violets blue as your eyes,
To the woody hollows in which we meet
    And the valleys of Paradise.

The slender acacia would not shake
    One long milk-bloom on the tree;
The white lake-blossom fell into the lake
    As the pimpernel dozed on the lea;
But the rose was awake all night for your sake,
    Knowing your promise to me;
The lilies and roses were all awake,
    They sigh'd for the dawn and thee.

Queen rose of the rosebud garden of girls,
    Come hither, the dances are done,
In gloss of satin and glimmer of pearls,
    Queen lily and rose in one;
Shine out, little head, sunning over with curls,
    To the flowers, and be their sun.

There has fallen a splendid tear
    From the passion-flower at the gate.
She is coming, my dove, my dear;
    She is coming, my life, my fate;
The red rose cries, 'She is near, she is near';
    And the white rose weeps, 'She is late';
The larkspur listens, 'I hear, I hear';
    And the lily whispers, 'I wait.'

She is coming, my own, my sweet;
    Were it ever so airy a tread,
My heart would hear her and beat,
    Were it earth in an earthy bed;
My dust would hear her and beat
    Had I lain for a century dead;
Would start and tremble under her feet,
    And blossom in purple and red.

FROM PART II

O that 'twere possible
After long grief and pain
To find the arms of my true love
Round me once again!

When I was wont to meet her
In the silent woody places
By the home that gave me birth,
We stood tranced in long embraces
Mixt with kisses sweeter sweeter
Than anything on earth.

A shadow flits before me,
Not thou, but like to thee:
Ah Christ, that it were possible
For one short hour to see
The souls we loved, that they might tell us
What and where they be.

It leads me forth at evening,
It lightly winds and steals
In a cold white robe before me,
When all my spirit reels
At the shouts, the leagues of lights,
And the roaring of the wheels.

Half the night I waste in sighs,
Half in dreams I sorrow after
The delight of early skies;
In a wakeful doze I sorrow
For the hand, the lips, the eyes,
For the meeting of the morrow,
The delight of happy laughter,
The delight of low replies.

'Tis a morning pure and sweet,
And a dewy splendour falls
On the little flower that clings
To the turrets and the walls;
'Tis a morning morning pure and sweet,
And the light and shadow fleet;
She is walking in the meadow,
And the woodland echo rings;
In a moment we shall meet;
She is singing in the meadow
And the rivulet at her feet
Ripples on in light and shadow
To the ballad that she sings.

Do I hear her sing as of old,
My bird with the shining head,
My own dove with the tender eye?
But there rings on a sudden a passionate cry,
There is some one dying or dead,
And a sullen thunder is roll'd;
For a tumult shakes the city,
And I wake, my dream is fled;
In the shuddering dawn, behold,
Without knowledge, without pity,
By the curtains of my bed
That abiding phantom cold.

THEODORE WATTS-DUNTON

The First Kiss

If only in dreams may Man be fully blest,
　　Is heaven a dream? Is she I claspt a dream?
　　Or stood she here even now where dew-drops gleam
And miles of furze shine yellow down the West?
I seem to clasp her still – still on my breast
　　Her bosom beats: I see the blue eyes beam.
　　I think she kiss'd these lips, for now they seem
Scarce mine: so hallow'd of the lips they press'd.

Yon thicket's breath – can that be eglantine?
　　Those birds – can they be Morning's choristers?
　　Can this be Earth? Can these be banks of furze? –
Like burning bushes fired of God they shine!
I seem to know them, though this body of mine
　　Pass'd into spirit at the touch of hers!

from *The Coming of Love*

A Dream

Beneath the loveliest dream there coils a fear:
  Last night came she whose eyes are memories now;
  Her far-off gaze seemed all-forgetful how
Love dimmed them once, so calm they shone and clear.
'Sorrow,' I said, 'has made me old, my dear;
  'Tis I, indeed, but grief can change the brow:
  Beneath *my* load a seraph's neck might bow,
Vigils like mine would blanch an angel's hair.'
Oh, then I saw, I saw the sweet lips move!
  I saw the love-mists thickening in her eyes –
I heard a sound as if a murmuring dove
  Felt lonely in the dells of Paradise;
But when upon my neck she fell, my love,
  Her hair smelt sweet of whin and woodland spice.

from *The Coming of Love*

Oscar Wilde

Requiescat

Tread lightly, she is near
    Under the snow,
Speak gently, she can hear
    The daisies grow.

All her bright golden hair
    Tarnished with rust,
She that was young and fair
    Fallen to dust.

Lily-like, white as snow,
    She hardly knew
She was a woman, so
    Sweetly she grew.

Coffin board, heavy stone,
    Lie on her breast,
I vex my heart alone,
    She is at rest.

Peace, peace, she cannot hear
    Lyre or sonnet,
All my life's buried here,
    Heap earth upon it.

Index of Titles

118

Index of First Lines